Today's Modern Day Princess

Girl's Journal

Doreen Hanna, Author

Contributions & Design

by Kara Ashbaugh

ISBN: 978-1468016161

Treasured Celebrations Ministries
1820 W. Carson Street #202-176
Torrance, CA 90501
310-533-9053

www.moderndayprincess.net

info@moderndayprincess.net

Printed in the United States of America

TABLE OF CONTENTS

Dedication and Acknowledgements

To my daughters

Brandy Danielle Corea & Kamy Gay Griffin.

My precious God-given gifts that have increased

my measure of faith, brought abundant blessings

into my life, and now walk beside me.

I look forward to all that God has for you, knowing that

"You have been born for such a time as this."

And to my loyal and faithful husband Chad;

who has believed in me and patiently supported this endeavor.

To my personal assistant, Kara Ashbaugh, and editor, Lorri Bradford;

I could not have done this without you.

May God's richest blessings be upon you both as this program

touches the lives of young girls across the US and internationally

because of you.

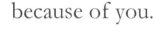

Session 1:
Discovering
the Princess Within

Princess Personality Profile

1	2	3	4
☐ I love to tell funny stories.	☐ When I am joking, sometimes people think I'm serious.	☐ I love to laugh, but not when it hurts someone's feelings.	☐ I can keep a straight face when being funny.
☐ I make quick decisions.	☐ I make decisions that are usually right.	☐ I make decisions based on all the facts.	☐ I don't like making decisions - Others can.
☐ I like lots of friends and being the center of attention.	☐ I like being the head of the group.	☐ I like being alone.	☐ I like to go with the flow.
☐ I like to talk a lot rather than listen.	☐ When I talk, people usually listen.	☐ I think carefully before I talk.	☐ I like to listen more than talk. Keeps me out of trouble.
☐ I'm very sociable and make tons of friends easily.	☐ I like to be in charge when I'm with my friends.	☐ I love having a few friends I know really well.	☐ I love to sit back and watch. I'm the quiet one in the group.
☐ I love excitement and change. I get bored easily.	☐ I like a good challenge.	☐ I like schedules and routines.	☐ I like variety- Knowing a little bit about a lot of things.
☐ I try to make everything fun.	☐ I get things done quickly and efficiently.	☐ I think and plan before I do something.	☐ I do things to be helpful and please others.
☐ If I were stranded on an island... I'd look for other people.	☐ If I were stranded on an island...I'd figure out how to get us rescued.	☐ If I were stranded on an island...I'd explore it.	☐ If I were stranded on an island...I'd relax and enjoy the beach.
Total____	Total____	Total____	Total____

Knowing Me ~ My Strengths and Weaknesses

Social Butterfly

Strengths
- Loves to talk
- Expressive
- Bubbly
- Funny
- Good storyteller
- Lives in the moment
- Enjoys people
- Creative
- Energetic
- Volunteers
- Inspires other

Weaknesses
- Forgetful
- Tends to exaggerate
- Doesn't like being serious
- Gullible and naïve
- Disorganized
- Leaves things unfinished

I Love...
- Attention
- Affection
- Approval
- Acceptance

Independent Leader

Strengths
- Born leader
- Loves to take charge
- Independent
- Self-sufficient
- Dynamic
- Active
- Is usually right
- Excels in emergencies
- Confident
- Quick worker
- Likes to set goals

Weaknesses
- Too controlling
- Insensitive
- Impatient
- Perceived as unfeeling
- Doesn't like to share credit
- Too focused, can't relax

I Love...
- Supportive people
- Being appreciated
- Abilities recognized
- Goals achieved

Organizational Queen

Strengths
- Organized
- Analytical
- Sensitive and thoughtful
- Has high standards
- Appreciates beauty
- Creative/Artistic
- Musical
- Conscientious
- Likes schedules
- Detailed
- Needs to finish things

Weaknesses
- Easily depressed
- Too sensitive
- Dwells on negatives
- Perfectionist
- Skeptical of others' motives
- Stresses over details

I Love...
- Stability
- Space
- Silence
- Sensitivity

Dependable Friend

Strengths
- Great listener
- Well liked
- Quiet
- Patient
- Calm, cool, and collected
- Dry sense of humor
- Sympathetic and kind
- Easy to get along with
- Dependable
- Consistent
- Peacemaker

Weaknesses
- Stubborn
- Not enough enthusiasm
- Compromises too often
- Indecisive
- Lacks energy
- Takes the easy way out

I Love...
- Peace and quiet
- Respect
- Being Valued
- Emotional support

Social Butterfly

I Hate…
- Budgets
- Deadlines
- Schedules
- Criticism
- Boredom
- "Stick in the mud's"

I Offer…
- Colorful creativity
- Optimism
- Entertainment
- A light touch

Independent Leader

I Hate…
- Messed up schedules
- Unproductive work
- Laziness
- Disloyalty
- Not being appreciated
- No independence

I Offer…
- Good time management
- Good judgment
- Fresh perspective
- Strong work ethic

Organizational Queen

I Hate…
- Making a mistake
- Being misunderstood
- Compromising
- Forgetfulness
- Being late
- Disorganization

I Offer…
- Sense of detail
- A love of analysis
- Great follow-through
- High standards

Dependable Friend

I Hate…
- Conflict
- Change
- Pushy people
- Loud music or talking
- People who think I'm not smart because I'm quiet

I Offer…
- Peace-making skills
- Objectivity
- Problem-solving skills
- A shoulder to cry on

Session 1 Project:

1) Look at the Personality Profile you took in class and list several personality traits that you like about yourself:

    a)_____

    b)_____

    c)_____

    d)_____

    e)_____

2) Which of the quotes on the next page do you like most? Place a star by it.

3) Your facilitator will provide you with 3 sealed envelopes for you to give to 3 trusted adults of your choice. Instructions are included in each envelope. After each of these trusted adults have completed what they are to do, have them return the **sealed** envelope to you before the next class. Do Not open them!!

4) Bring the sealed envelopes to our next class together.

5) Choose your favorite quote from "Quotes to Ponder" on the next page.

Quotes to Ponder

"A girl's self-image is the core of her personality. It affects every aspect of her behavior: the ability to learn, the capacity to grow and change. A positive self-image is the best possible preparation for success in life."

Dr. Joyce Brothers

"Having a purpose in life is determined by what you make of life and what you make of yourself."

Submitted by Teresita P., Age 15 --- Hawaii
Motivational Quotes from Teens; Motivateus.com

"You must love yourself before you can love another. By accepting yourself and fully being what you are, your simple presence can make others happy."

Anonymous

"Personality has the power to open many doors, but **character** must keep them open."
~ Anonymous

Session 2:
My Legacy
Empowers My Destiny

DO YOU KNOW WHO?

She was born on January 29, 1954 in Koscusko, Mississippi. Her parents' names were Vernita Lee and Vernon. They were never married. Her dad, Vernon, who was twenty years old at the time of her birth, was in the Army. Sometime after their little girl was born, Vernita Lee moved to Milwaukee, Wisconsin, to look for a better job leaving her little girl with her husband's mother (the little girl's grandmother) who lived on a farm and had no indoor plumbing. Her grandmother loved going to church so this girl spent much of her time in church. By the age of 3, she was reading the Bible and reciting it publicly in church.

She went to live with her mother at the age of 6. By the age of 13, after suffering abuse and molestation, she ran away and was sent to a juvenile detention home only to be denied admission because all the beds were filled. When she was fourteen she gave birth to a premature baby that died shortly thereafter. As a last resort, she was sent to Nashville to live under her father's strict discipline. He saw to it that his daughter met a midnight curfew, and he required her to read a book and write a book report each week.

When she turned nineteen, she got her first broadcasting job at WVOL in Nashville in 1972. She became the first black anchorwoman at Nashville's WTVF-TV, then moved to Baltimore in 1976. After being co-anchor at WJZ-TV for two years, she was hired to host the station's chat show, People Are Talking.

CAN YOU GUESS YET?

In 1984, after eight years at WJZ, she became the host of A.M. Chicago. In 1985, she received an Oscar Nomination for Best Supporting Actress in the movie The Color Purple.

In 1986, "The Oprah Winfrey Show" became the number one talk show in national syndication in less than a year. She was the youngest person and only the fifth woman ever to receive the honor in IRTS's 25-year history.

In 1991, motivated in part by her own memories of childhood abuse, she initiated a campaign to establish a national database of convicted child abusers, and testified before a U.S. Senate Judiciary Committee on behalf of a National Child Protection Act

When *Forbes* magazine published its list of America's billionaires for the year 2003, it disclosed that Oprah Winfrey was the first African-American woman to become a billionaire.

Oprah Winfrey

DO YOU KNOW WHO?

When I was born, I was immediately put on a respirator - a tube was inserted into my chest to help me breathe. My mother wept. My birth father, Vernon, left the hospital and went to the parking lot to get drunk.

Before I turned 3 years old we left Vernon and moved with only the clothes on our backs and stayed with one of Mom's friends. I began calling this woman Nanny. Mom and I slept on a mattress in Nanny's living room between the front door and the kitchen. She hung a tarp around the bed so we'd have privacy.

Ours was not the ideal situation for a kid growing up but my mother made it work. She never told me if we had money problems or how depressed she felt. My mom's way of coping was always turning on Country Western music and she always encouraged me to sing with her.

Vernon (my Dad) had scheduled visitations every other weekend but I always was afraid to be around him. He would pick me up and then go directly to the video rental store to pick up 4 or 5 videos. We'd to his house; I'd pop the videos while he'd sit and play solitaire till he fell asleep in his chair. In between videos, I'd cook my own frozen dinners – that was our weekend.

When I was 6 my mother remarried. Her new husband was Ray Parker. A year later she had my brother Brett. We lived a bit above poverty level. Mom would always say "You don't need to be rich to be happy." I remember Mom used to proudly walk in and out of the discount stores. I'd be so embarrassed, now at the age of 12, that I wouldn't even carry the bag. Mom would say, "Fine, I'll carry it.

Son, poverty is no reason for shame. What you wear doesn't matter. Who you <u>are</u> does."

Until I was 8, I would call Vernon and ask him to pick me up but things began to change —I decided I'd try and wait for him to call. First I waited 2 or 3 months then I'd call. Then 8 or 9 months and I'd call him again. No matter how long I waited, he never called me. This went on until I turned 16. When I got my driver's license I called Vernon and told him that I'd like to spend some time with him. I told him to call me when he wanted me to come. He never called and I never went to see him again.

One thing Vernon did was send me a birthday card every year. For many years it was the only contact we had. They were always signed on the inside – "Daddy." I remember opening those cards and I would want to be so angry. I would want to laugh about them, to ridicule how stupid they were, and pretend they didn't matter to me, but in some way they did. They meant in some way that he still cared.

I have learned that you can't force people to feel things they aren't willing to feel. Not everyone will love you the way you want them to. Those people often times are lonely because they build walls instead of bridges, like my father.

Living with my step-father, Ray, I always felt awkward in his presence. He had 3 kids of his own by his first marriage and I was his only stepchild. By the time I was in high school things it was evident he didn't want me around. Brett could get away with anything he wanted to, I couldn't.

One day Ray said my room smelled like dirty shoes because I never cleaned it up. I looked around and he had hidden stink bombs under my bed. He would mow the yard in squiggly lines and then make me mow it after him. He would take things off my bookshelf, throw them on the floor and then tell me I was messy. On day he said the whole family was going to take a ride in my step-sister's new car. I was so excited. But he said "No. You have to clean out the freezer." They all drove away and left me there.

Then I left for college, and about the same time Ray became ill. As he lay dying in the hospital I struggled. I guess I still secretly wanted him to be my father, so I could call him Dad and mean it. I wanted someone to be proud to call me son. Before he died in he called everyone into his room days before his passing to say good-bye to everyone but me. My only hope was that I had seen him less selfish in his last days and I actually felt compassion for him. I chose to plan his funeral and sang for it.

Recently my mom said that before Ray died, a friend had stopped at the hospital to see him. He said to his friend, "I'm proud of my son Brett, he is going to join the military and grow into a fine man. Then he looked out the window and said "and my other son is going to be a famous singer one day, he has the most beautiful voice."

After a few summers I was recruited to join the largest branch of the YMCA, Jeff the director, became my mentor. I admired Jeff's steady leadership. He was an authority figure (much like a dad) with heart and that inspired me. He taught me the importance of servant leadership. I finished at the YMCA and went to college at the University of North Carolina and got a part time job helping a family with a child with a disability.

I was assigned to single mother with a son who had autism. Diane heard me singing around her house one day and told me she'd been watching a show called American Idol and that I should apply next season. She found out the next season they would be auditioning in Charlotte, NC. I went and didn't make it. Then Diane prompted me to audition in Atlanta. The rest is history, I was the 3rd in line for American Idol - Kelly Clarkson was the winner. But, my singing career has been sent to the moon, as well as my non-profit organization for disabled kids. I learned that my looks didn't matter – my talent did. Thousands of votes on American Idol said to me "Looks don't matter. Self-respect and using my talent does."

My priority in life today is not having a hit song- but setting a good example. There is a difference between image and appearance. Appearance is God-given and we make the best of it. But your image comes from what you do. I realize that God placed me into every situation that led me where I am today to shape me into a better servant. I didn't get this singing voice to make myself famous and rich. It is to become a better messenger.

Remember…

Be willing to take risks.

Failing doesn't hurt; Not trying does.

Listen to your heart.

The great glory never comes from winning, but from rising when you fall.

Stand up for what you believe in.

We are all born with Gifts.

I have struggled but I have also had satisfaction

I have been abandoned, but I have been loved.

I have lost many more times than I've won.

A person is defined by what he chooses to do with their life, not by what happens to them.

Clay Aiken

Session 2 Project:

Explore your family's heritage!

1) How many generations back can your family remember? (Complete the family tree on pg.29)

2) Is there a favorite family story or tradition that has been passed down from generation to generation? (Use page 30 to record any you discover)

3) What is your nationality? Italian, Hispanic, Irish, etc.

4) Does your family name (your last name) have special meaning?

5) What does your first name mean?

6) Read and choose your favorite "Quotes to Ponder" for this session.

Bring back your discoveries next week.

Quotes to Ponder

"Call it a clan, call it a network, call it a tribe, call it a family. Whatever you call it, whoever you are, you need one."
~Jane Howard

"Parents can only give good advice or put their children on the right paths, but the final forming of a person's character lies in their own hands."
Anne Frank

"It is not flesh and blood but the heart which makes us family."

~Johann Schiller

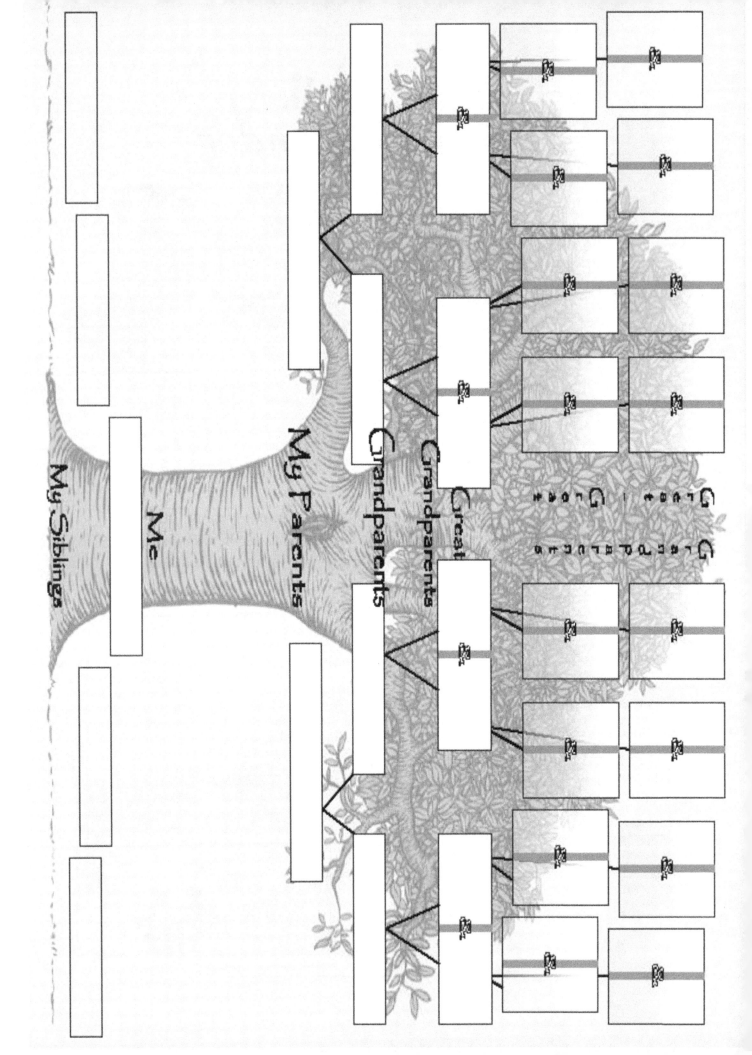

Today's
Modern Day Princess

My Last Name (family name) is _____

It means _____

My nationality, culture, &/or heritage is: _____

Stories &/or information I have learned about my family include: _____

Session 3:
The Wealth
Found in Obedience

Session 3 Project:

My Mom and Other Women in My Life

1) Write the qualities that you like in your mother & why:

Write an affirmation card to your mom – like the ones you received – and tell her the character traits you admire and appreciate in her. Then hide the card somewhere she will find it unexpectedly. (Inside the coffee container, her purse, makeup bag, or car's sun visor.) Just be sure she WILL find it! ☺

2) Who is another woman (or women) in your life that you look up to and ask advice from? Why?

3) Read and choose your favorite "Quotes to Ponder" for this session.

Quotes to Ponder

"Biology is the least of what makes someone a mother."
~ Oprah Winfrey

"A daughter is a mother's gender partner, often her closest ally in the family, an extension of herself. Mothers are their daughters' role model; the trendsetter of all their relationships."
~ Victoria Secunda

"There is no shame in taking orders from those who have learned to obey."
~ William Forster

"EVERY GREAT PERSON HAS LEARNED TO OBEY, WHOM TO OBEY AND WHEN TO OBEY."

~ WILLIAM A. HOWARD

"Obedience is better than sacrifice."
The NIV

Session 4:
The Portrait
of a Man of Integrity

Session 4 Project:

1) Complete the following as you study the qualities of a man of integrity with your facilitator:

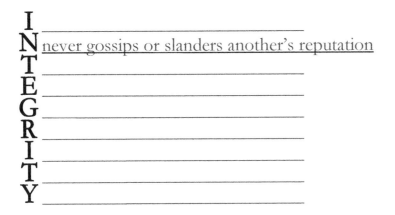

I _____
N never gossips or slanders another's reputation
T _____
E _____
G _____
R _____
I _____
T _____
Y _____

2) This week fill out the following page entitled "The Men in My Life." (Next page)

3) Write a note to the man you most respect and state one or two of the qualities you most appreciate about him. For example, is he trustworthy, forgiving, or kind?

4) Read and choose your favorite "Quotes to Ponder" for this session.

The Men in My Life

Write the qualities that you admire in the man you most respect in your life & why:

Who is another man in your life that you look up to and ask advice from? Why?

What are the qualities that you would like to see in a future boyfriend or husband?

Quotes to Ponder

"A man who walks with integrity speaks truth from his heart."

~ The Message

Nothing is more sacred than the integrity of your own mind.
~ Ralph Waldo Emerson

With courage you will dare to take risks, have the strength to be compassionate, and the wisdom to be humble. Courage is the foundation of integrity.
~ Keshavan Nair

Six essential qualities that are the key to success: Sincerity, personal integrity, humility, courtesy, wisdom, charity.
~ William Menninger

Session 5:
The Treasure
of True Friends

QUOTES ON FRIENDSHIP FROM THE "TEEN HEALTH" WEBSITE

For Ashley, it was like this: She was sitting with a big group in the school lunchroom when she accidentally knocked her drink onto her lap. As word spread that it looked like Ashley had wet herself, the laughter began to mount. Then she noticed her best friend doing something strange.

"She poured water on herself," Ashley said.

True friendship is hard to find, Ashley says. But she knows it when she sees it. And so do many of you. We asked our readers what it takes to be a good friend. The responses poured in — more than 5,000 of you sent us emails.

For some, the defining moments of friendship were profound, such as the soulmate who helps you through the grief of losing a family member or camps out in your hospital room when you're sick. For others, it's smaller gestures that loom large — the friend who talks for hours when you're feeling alone, even if it means going over on her cell phone minutes; the one who helps you with your homework, even when she hasn't done her own; or the friend who helps you search for your retainer, even when it means going through the garbage from the school lunch.

Acts of Friendship

Big or small, it's the **actions** that seem to count the most in friendship. In a time when we can chat effortlessly by IM, text, and email, talk is getting cheaper. Many of you believe that the evidence of true friends is what they *do* to show their loyalty, honesty, trustworthiness, or willingness to make a sacrifice when you need help.

Kaitlin, 14, told us about a friend who took the blame for her when she got in a fight at school. Her friend was suspended for 10 days.

"I got sick, and my friend ran to the bathroom after me to hold my hair back as I became the Exorcist," Marissa said. "She stood by me, while my other 'friend' yelled at me to get off the floor and clean it up."

And it works both ways: Nearly three quarters of the people who wrote to us said they do as much for their friends as their friends do for them. Sometimes the most treasured acts of friendship are those for which you expect to get nothing in return, not even credit for a good deed.

"The nicest thing I ever did for a friend was when I let her date my ex — without ever telling her that I was against it," Rae'Johne, 14, said.

Elaina, 15, remembers the day she went clothes shopping with her best friend, who is overweight. The saleslady was being rude to her friend because there was so little in her size and nothing fit quite right. Elaina is proud of how she helped her friend that day. "I had like an armful of clothes for myself (and may I add these clothes were to DIE for!) and I put all my clothes back and said, 'I don't like what they have in here, why don't we go somewhere with better clothes, not these cheap ones.'"

Session 5 Project:

Most Important Qualities In a Friend
List qualities you consider when choosing a friend:

1) Turn to the page entitled "My Friends". Think about 3 of your closest friendship. Write down the qualities you appreciate about each friend and answer the questions.

2) When you complete the questions, write a note to the friend you appreciate most, sharing what you love about her and how much you appreciate having her in your life.

3) Do you have any regrets about past friendships?

4) What things do you need to work on in yourself to be a better friend?

5) Choose your favorite quote from "Quotes to Ponder".

My Friends

Her Picture Here!

My friend's name:

What I like about my friend:

One thing I would change about our relationship to make it better:

My Friends

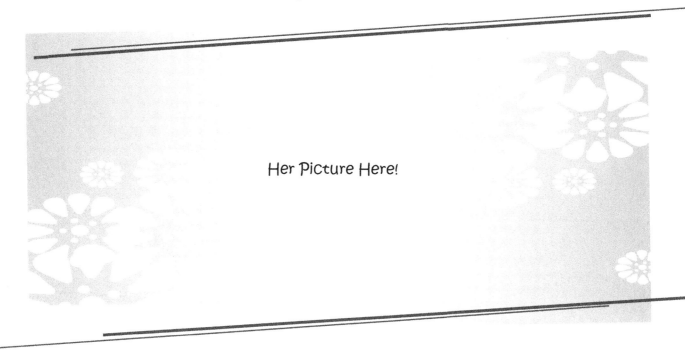

Her Picture Here!

My friend's name:

What I like about my friend:

One thing I would change about our relationship to make it better:

My Friends

Her Picture Here!

My friend's name:

What I like about my friend:

One thing I would change about our relationship to make it better:

Quotes to Ponder

"Without friends no one would want to live, even if he had all of life's riches."
~ Aristotle

"... pay all your debts except the debt of love for your friends, never finish paying that!"
LB

"A real friend will tell you when you have spinach stuck in your teeth"
~ Author Unknown

Session 6:
Enhancing the
Beauty of a Princess

Session 6 Project:

Tips I learned and want to remember about:

Makeup:

Manners:

Choose your favorite quote from "Quotes to Ponder".

Be sure to fill out the page entitled "My Favorites" and give a copy your facilitator today!

My Favorites Sheet

Name:_____

My Favorite Flower:_____

Favorite thing in Nature:
(ocean, the moon, the stars, a river, a mountain, etc.)

_____

_____

_____

_____

My Favorite Animal & why:

_____

_____

_____

_____

My Favorite Food:

_____

_____

My Favorite Place To Go:

_____

_____

_____

My Favorite Song & why:

_____

_____

_____

Quotes to Ponder

"There is no cosmetic for beauty like happiness."
~ Countess of Blessington, Marguerite Gardiner

"Personal beauty is a better recommendation than a letter of reference."

~ Aristotle

"People are like stained-glass windows. They sparkle and shine when the sun is out, but when the darkness sets in their true beauty is revealed only if there is light from within. "
~Elisabeth Kübler-Ross

"CULTIVATE INNER BEAUTY, THE GENTLE AND GRACIOUS KIND THAT GOD DELIGHTS IN."

~ THE MESSAGE

Session 7:
Beginning to
Act Like a Princess

Mother Theresa

"I came from a poor family of ten children. The sisters who taught me in grades 1-3 were very good to me and made a favorable impression on me. They helped me and yet didn't make me feel less than the other children in school who probably had more material things in life than I. From that time on, I always remained close to the sisters and thought the Lord was calling me to minister to orphan children.

When I was a freshman in high school, I visited the novitiate of the Grey Nuns in Lowell, Massachusetts where I lived. I thought if I were to enter religious life, this is where I would go. These were the only sisters I knew.

In my sophomore year of high school, in a surprise turn of events, I went to St. Anne's Orphanage in Methuen, Massachusetts and attended St. Theresa's High School. This was the first time I lived outside of the city of Lowell.

The Good Shepherd Sisters taught at this school. This was my first exposure to these sisters and I knew then, this is where God was calling me! Why else did He make it possible for me to get to know these sisters?

I kept in contact with the sisters and in 1950, when I graduated from Salem High School, I asked for my admission into this religious community. I was advised to wait a year as I was rather frail and sickly. I worked a year and finally, in September of 1951, I entered the Good Shepherd Sisters in Bay View. Before the end of my second year of training in the novitiate, the superiors told me that I was too sickly to become a sister. It was a sad day when I left the convent. I questioned my vocation! However, I told myself that I would return!

I waited, prayed, and kept my faith. Since I still felt the call to religious life, I asked to re-enter the convent. The permission to re-enter was granted to me and to three other women. When it came time for my religious profession a year later, I was the only one remaining since the other three women had left during the year. Why did God choose me and not them? In a family of ten children, why was I the one called to religious life?

My family was supportive of my decision but some questioned why I would want to shut myself up in the convent. On February 15, 1955, I pronounced my first vows as a religious in the Congregation of the Servants of the Immaculate Heart of Mary, better known as the Good Shepherd Sisters of Quebec.

In my 48 years of vowed life, I could tell you many stories of how God directed my life, how he put the right people at the right time in my life, and how events happened at the time they did because God had plans for me. My goal in life has always been to do God's will, wherever he called me, however he called me, and for whatever time he wanted me in a certain place or ministry.

There has been much variety in my life. I have been housemother, student, teacher, principal, superior, counselor, social worker in two nursing homes, and Adoption Worker at St. Andre Home.
I never regretted my decision to become religious I pray each day that I may live out my passion and commitment to the best of my ability.

~ **Mother Theresa**

Session 7 Project:

1) Each day this week, you will be writing a short entry in your "Journal of My Feelings".
   a) First thing in the morning, write down how you are feeling. Then think about the things we have discussed in this session. How are you going to approach the situation that's on your mind today: by walking in your core belief or just by the way you are feeling?
   b) In the evening write down how you may have responded differently today because you chose not to give into your feelings ~ or because you did ~ then write what happened.

2) Complete the Celebration Bio sheet and give to your facilitator.

3) Choose your favorite quote for this session and try to memorize it!

Quotes to Ponder

"It's faith in something and enthusiasm for it that makes a life worth living."

~ Wendell Holmes

"Without faith, nothing is possible. With it, nothing is impossible."

~ Mary McLeod Bethune & The Message

"The best and most beautiful things in the world cannot be seen, nor touched ... but are felt in the heart."

~ Helen Keller

"A faith that moves mountains is a faith that expands horizons. It does not bring us into a smaller world of easy answers; but into a larger one where there is room to wonder."

~ Rich Mullins

"YOU CANNOT MAKE YOURSELF FEEL SOMETHING YOU DO NOT FEEL, BUT YOU CAN MAKE YOURSELF DO RIGHT IN SPITE OF YOUR FEELINGS."

~ PEARL S. BUCK

Journal of My Feelings

Day 1

This morning I'm feeling:

Because:

Today, I can choose to be:

Because:

_____

Tonight, as I look back on my day, I see that I chose:

Journal of My Feelings

Day 2

This morning I'm feeling:

Because:

Today, I can choose to be:

Because:

_____

Tonight, as I look back on my day, I see that I chose:

Day 3

This morning I'm feeling:

Because:

Today, I can choose to be:

Because:

Tonight, as I look back on my day, I see that I chose:

Journal of My Feelings

Day 4

This morning I'm feeling:

Because:

Today, I can choose to be:

Because:

_____

Tonight, as I look back on my day, I chose:

Journal of My Feelings

Day 5

This morning I'm feeling:

Because:

Today, I can choose to be:

Because:

Tonight, as I look back on my day, I chose:

Day 6

This morning I'm feeling:

Because:

Today, I can choose to be:

Because:

_____

Tonight, as I look back on my day, I chose:

Day 7

This morning I'm feeling:

Because:

Today, I can choose to be:

Because:

Tonight, as I look back on my day, I chose:

BIOGRAPHY FOR MY NIGHT OF CELEBRATION"

NAME: _____

BORN ON: _____ IN (CITY & STATE): _____

PARENTS' NAMES: _____

MY NAME MEANS: _____

QUALITIES IN ME THAT OTHERS LOVE ARE (READ NOTE CARDS FROM WEEK 1):

_____

_____

_____

_____

✴ ✴

(THIS SECTION IS FOR YOUR LEADER TO WRITE IN.)

GIVE 1 OR 2 BRIEF COMMENTS ON THE GOOD QUALITIES AND/OR GROWTH YOU SAW IN THIS

GIRL AS SHE WENT THROUGH THE CLASS.

_____

_____

_____

_____

_____

Your

Celebration

Memories from
My Night of Celebration

Date:

Who gave my public blessing:

What I remember most about the words that were spoken about me:

My favorite part of the ceremony:

People that attended:

Other favorite memories:

Memories from
My Night of Celebration

Use this page for pictures!